DARTMOOI

A Pocket Guide

© Janet & Ossie Palmer

ORCHARD PUBLICATIONS
2 Orchard Close, Chudleigh, Newton Abbot, Devon TQ13 0LR
Telephone: 01626 852714

ISBN   9781898964841

Printed by Hedgerow Print
Crediton, Devon EX17 1ES

CONTENTS

FOR YOUR COMFORT AND SAFETY

The maps at the start of each sector are intended as a simple guide only and, from a practical point of view, we suggest that an Ordnance Survey Outdoor Leisure 28 map accompanies you at all times. This gives the names of all the major tors, shows the footpaths and bridleways and all the minor roads, most important if you choose to widen your explorations or take a wrong turning.

Strong shoes and a waterproof jacket are recommended for all your walks on the moor.

Guard Against Theft! Whenever you leave your car, take your valuables with you (credit cards, cash etc) – leave nothing visible in the car to encourage a break-in.

To check firing times on Military Ranges -
Freephone 0800 4584868. Website: www.dartmoor-ranges.co.uk

USEFUL INFORMATION

The Dartmoor National Park, Parke, Haytor Road, Bovey Tracey TQ13 9JQ 01626 832093. Their website - www.dartmoor-npa.gov.uk contains a vast amount of interesting information concerning Dartmoor and has links to many other National Park and Devon websites.

Dartmoor National Park Visitor/Information Centres

You will find a visit to one of these Centres well worthwhile. Maps, compasses and a comprehensive range of books and leaflets about Dartmoor can all be found here, plus a friendly, well-informed staff who will answer all your queries. They are situated at Haytor, Newbridge and Postbridge — open between Easter and October approximately.

The High Moorland Visitor Centre, Princetown 01822 890414 - Open all the year round. Facilities here include an interactive computerised history of the Moor, visual displays giving information on tin mining and the Moor as an Army Training ground, and an audio visual theatre. Talks on all aspects of Dartmoor are given here from time to time. Email: hmvc@dartmoor-npa.gov.co.uk

Interesting websites: www.legendarydartmoor.co.uk

INTRODUCTION

Swept by the most extreme elements of our English weather, Dartmoor's granite tors provide a marked contrast to the rich and gentle contours of Devon which surround them. Born in the primeval melting pot beneath the earth, they are the remnant core of an ancient range of mountains, their weird and wonderful stacks shaped over the millennia by heat and cold, wind and rain.

For several thousand years, man has inhabited the moor and granite from the tumbled stacks which litter the hillsides has been used in the construction of homes. Remnants of hut circles from 2,000 to 3,000 BC are numerous, whilst the ruins of ancient farms rub shoulders with their modern counterparts.

Here, set amidst our modern, highly technological world is an evocative and dramatic landscape, touched but untamed by the hand of man. It is a land full of legend and mystery but a land made accessible to all in the last decades through the creation of the Dartmoor National Park.

For visitors perhaps the most striking aspect of the Dartmoor landscape is the tors themselves. Opinions vary as to their number or, sometimes, even their proper name and this little book is not intended to be a scholarly or definitive work on these wonderful rock stacks. To list them all here would be impossible. Within these pages we have aimed simply to introduce them and to hope that, as you follow the excursions, your curiousity and interest will be aroused and that the time you spend in this very special part of England will prove to be a journey of discovery into Dartmoor itself.

EXCURSIONS THROUGH WEST DARTMOOR

WESTERN SECTOR MAP

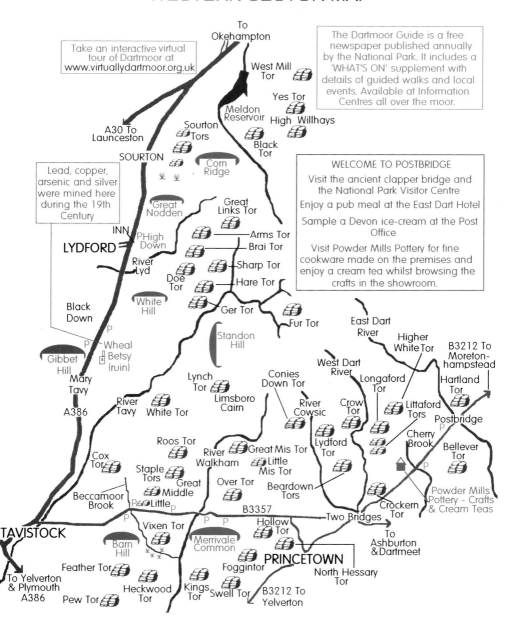

Take an interactive virtual tour of Dartmoor at www.virtuallydartmoor.org.uk

The Dartmoor Guide is a free newspaper published annually by the National Park. It includes a 'WHAT'S ON' supplement with details of guided walks and local events. Available at Information Centres all over the moor.

To Okehampton

West Mill Tor

Yes Tor

High Willhays

Meldon Reservoir

Sourton Tors

A30 To Launceston

SOURTON

Corn Ridge

Black Tor

Lead, copper, arsenic and silver were mined here during the 19th Century

Great Nodden

Great Links Tor

WELCOME TO POSTBRIDGE

Visit the ancient clapper bridge and the National Park Visitor Centre

Enjoy a pub meal at the East Dart Hotel

Sample a Devon ice-cream at the Post Office

Visit Powder Mills Pottery for fine cookware made on the premises and enjoy a cream tea whilst browsing the crafts in the showroom.

INN

P High Down

LYDFORD

River Lyd

Arms Tor

Brai Tor

Sharp Tor

Doe Tor

Hare Tor

White Hill

Ger Tor

Fur Tor

East Dart River

Higher White Tor

B3212 To Moreton-hampstead

Black Down

P

Wheal Betsy (ruin)

Standon Hill

West Dart River

Longaford Tor

Hartland Tor

Gibbet Hill

Mary Tavy

A386

River Tavy

White Tor

Lynch Tor

Limsboro Cairn

Conies Down Tor

River Cowsic

Crow Tor

Littaford Tors

Postbridge

P

Roos Tor

River Walkham

Great Mis Tor

Lydford Tor

Cherry Brook

Bellever Tor

Cox Tor

Staple Tors

Great Middle Little

Little Mis Tor

Over Tor

Beardown Tors

Powder Mills Pottery - Crafts & Cream Teas

Beccamoor Brook

P

Crockern Tor

B3357

Hollow Tor

Two Bridges

To Ashburton & Dartmeet

TAVISTOCK

Vixen Tor

Merrivale Common

PRINCETOWN

Barn Hill

Fogrintor

North Hessary Tor

To Yelverton & Plymouth A386

Feather Tor

Heckwood Tor

Kings Tor

Swell Tor

B3212 To Yelverton

Pew Tor

3

This excursion begins in the market town of Tavistock, an excellent base for exploring Dartmoor. Leave the town by the A386, travelling north towards Okehampton. The road winds along beside the River Tavy and beyond the Trout & Tipple pub, Smeardon Down dominates the skyline ahead with glimpses of Cox Tor on the right. Gibbet Hill forms a backdrop for the village of Mary Tavy and the road then climbs steadily upwards, entering a stretch of fenced moorland as it crosses Black Down.

Gibbet Hill is on the left and is easily reached on foot via one of the parking areas where gates give access to the moor. Its sinister name is well-earned as once upon a time many a felon met his end on the gibbet here and his remains were left hanging in an iron cage as a warning to others. No horrors spoil the view here today, just a succession of magnificent tors which march along Dartmoor's western edge. From the south, Cox Tor and the Staple Tor ridge ending in Roos Tor stretch northwards. The television mast on North Hessary Tor spikes the sky to the right of Roos Tor. White Tor is to the left of Roos, whilst further north the cliff-like form of Ger Tor stands above the entrance to beautiful Tavy Cleave. To the right of it, on a day when the atmosphere is crystal clear, remote and mysterious Fur Tor can be seen in the far distance.

Next in line stands chunky Hare Tor with conical Sharp Tor beyond and last in this line, but by no means least, is the multi-turreted Great Links Tor with the miniature stack of Little Links Tor on the side. These tors dwarf those on their lower slopes, rendering them indistinct on all but the clearest of days, but a much more interesting view can be seen from our detour further along the road.

The road leaves the high ground, dipping to cross the pretty valley of the River Lyd, and then climbs to the Dartmoor Inn, giving glimpses of moorland beyond the hedges. Immediately beyond the inn's car park a short trackway bears right to a gateway leading to the large parking area on High Down. Much of Dartmoor is used by farmers to graze their livestock and it is imperative that gates such as this one are kept shut to prevent these animals from straying onto the roads.

Before you even leave your car, Brai or Brat Tor with Widgery Cross on its summit dominates the eastern skyline and a short walk towards it across the central grassy trackway will bring you to a bench seat, an excellent place to stop and admire the scenery. Seen from far and near, the granite cross on this formidable tor makes it a landmark in this part of Dartmoor. Made of granite blocks, it was erected by artist William Widgery to celebrate the Golden Jubilee of Queen Victoria in 1887. On the right hand or south side of the tor the Doe Tor Brook tumbles down to meet the River Lyd, presently out of sight beneath the hill. Beyond it stands Doe Tor, dwarfed by Sharp Tor and Hare Tor which command the ridge behind it.

Widgery Cross, Brai Tor

On the days when Wilsworthy Range is being used for training, red flags will be flying from Doe and Hare Tors.

A dip in the ridge to the left of Brai Tor climbs to Arms Tor and from the bench it is possible to determine one of the rock stacks of Great Links Tor behind it. Several years ago, on a day in early October, Ossie and I climbed to Great Links from Arms Tor on a sunny afternoon to find every ledge of every rock stack massed with martins, gathering for the flight south for the winter. The noise of their chattering was incredible and, thousands at a time, they took flight, swooping and weaving around the rocks before settling once more upon the ledges. We watched them, fascinated, and learned later from a knowledgeable friend that it must be an annual gathering place for them as their next point south was Berry Head, near Brixham which is visible from Great Links on a clear day.

Great Nodden is the name of the plum-pudding hill on the far left and the tiny dot on top is a cairn, one of many on the Dartmoor hills. A short distance from the bench all paths dip to the beautiful valley of the River Lyd which is crossed by a sturdy clam or stepping stones should you wish to continue your explorations here.

River Lyd

Great Nodden is predominant beyond the hedges as you continue your journey along the A386 towards Okehampton. At the hamlet of Sourton you will find convenient parking opposite the Highwayman Inn close to tiny Sourton Church. Beside the church a trackway goes to the moor over a little bridge. It once crossed the railway line between Okehampton and Tavistock but now National Cycle Route 27 runs beneath it, providing a super route for walkers and cyclists. The section which runs along the edge of western Dartmoor is known as the Granite Way. In front of you a 'stroll' between enclosure walls leads up to the spikey peaks of the Sourton Tors whilst paths high and low traverse the common towards Great Nodden with spectacular views over the countryside.

Continue towards Okehampton and just after the petrol station and motel turn right onto the A30 dual carriageway, leaving it at the Okehampton junction a short distance away. This short stretch of dual carriageway gives you a fine view of West Mill Tor with the Yes Tor, High Willhays ridge to the right of it. From the sliproad, Okehampton is just a short distance away along the B3260 but two diversions might be of interest to you.

From the end of the slip road turn right, taking the road to Meldon and the Reservoir, and later branch left for the Reservoir. Completed in 1972, the reservoir effectively drowned a spectacular stretch of the West Okement River but the artificial lake thus created carries a classic beauty all its own. As you crest the hill there is a fine view of the deep cleft of the West Okement gorge with the multiple stacks of Black Tor high above it. Meldon Reservoir has a large car park with an information board on the industries which once flourished in this valley. There are walks into the valley and around the reservoir perimeter. Meldon Viaduct is a dominating feature in the landscape below the dam and it is possible to walk to it through the valley.

Meldon Reservoir

An alternative route would be to return along the Meldon/Reservoir road to the bridge just below the point where you branched off left to the reservoir. Just below the bridge there is limited parking at the side of the road and a short walk back up the hill will bring you on the right to an access point on the Granite Way which we mentioned earlier. This route makes use of what was once the railway track from Okehampton to Tavistock which crossed the West Okement Gorge by way of Meldon Viaduct. Turn right to cross the bridge over the road where you parked your car. A walk of about half a mile along this tarmac path will bring you to the Viaduct and a magnificent view. Looking down into the valley from the far end of the Viaduct you will see Meldon Dam, although the Reservoir itself is hidden from view behind the hill. The hill in the far distance is Corn Ridge and the 'pimple' on it is a rock stack known as Branscombe's Loaf. On the left hand side of the dam rises Longstone Hill with Yes Tor towering above it, although High Willhays is just out of sight along the ridge. The tor to the left of Yes Tor is West Mill Tor.

Yes Tor from Meldon Quarry car park

Before we finish this journey yet another short excursion is possible from the road to Okehampton. This time turn left at the end of the sliproad from the A30 and continue towards Okehampton. Opposite Betty Cottles Inn take the little road which goes up to Meldon Quarry. This narrow but picturesque road winds through Meldon Woods, a scene of great beauty in bluebell time. Essentially it is the quarry road so be prepared for lorries but the public road ends at a car park which gives access to walks into the West Okement valley and its bygone industries which are illustrated on the Information Board in the car park. Close by the Red-a-ven Brook tumbles to its confluence with the East Okement. Its source lies beneath the craggy height of Yes Tor which is perfectly framed by the hills above the car park.

Once again our exploration begins in Tavistock, but this time follow the signs from the town centre along the B3357 towards Princetown. As the road climbs towards the moor, Cox Tor dominates the skyline but once across the cattle grid a large expanse of open moorland and some formidable tors come quickly into view. Our first stopping place is Barn Hill car park on the right hand side of the road where the panoramic views across Tavistock to the distant hills of Bodmin Moor are breath-taking. Southwards gleams Plymouth Sound, the bridge across the Tamar and the English Channel. This is part of the area that Ossie and I patrol as Voluntary Wardens for the National Park and the views go a long way to compensate for the onerous task of collecting litter which, wind-blown or otherwise, seems to gather in the bracken on the hill.

Looking northwest off the moor, the conical peak with a building on the top is Brentor, an ancient volcanic plug with a tiny church at its summit. Directly in front is Cox Tor, whilst across Beckamoore Coombe the lowly pile of Little Staple Tor clings to the side of the ridge. Next in line is Middle Staple Tor but it is the weird shapes of the rock stacks on Great Staple Tor which draw the eye, each one looking as if a puff of wind could send the enormous rocks tumbling down. All are easily accessible from the car parks along this road.

Great Staple Tor

We suggest however that you turn to the south and follow one of the many pathways which cross the short turf of Barn Hill until you reach a series of low rock stacks looking out over the saddle of the hill beyond. Prominent in the foreground to the left of the scene is Vixen Tor, Dartmoor's tallest rock stack and one that seems to change its shape from whichever direction you view it. According to legend a wicked witch inhabits the tor, conjuring dense mists to lure travellers into the bog which lies at its foot. On its far side flows the River Walkham, whilst beyond the river the ground rises steadily across Merrivale Common to Hollow Tor and the tall mast on North Hessary Tor, a landmark visible from many points on the moor.

Vixen Tor

On the skyline to the right of the mast is Kings Tor where the ridge stretches back to Swell Tor and the quarry spoiltips below. Granite was quarried in this area for many years in the 19th and early 20th centuries and remnants of that industry are a feature in the landscape. The railway tracks that served them now form part of the cycleways and walking routes on this part of the moor. Next right is the long hill with the multi stacks of Leedon Tor which overshadow Ingra Tor on the lower skyline. Recognisable by its point is Sharpitor with the long shoulder of Peek Hill beside it. Below it, much nearer to hand and this side of the River Walkham, are the tumbled rocks of Heckwood Tor with a tree or two close to its summit. Closer still is Feather Tor and, across the leat which flows beneath it, stands the medieval cross known as Windy Post.

Dominating the skyline on the right of your view here is Pew Tor, perhaps a favourite of ours because of its proximity to home. Here with around two thousand others in August 1999, we watched as the shadow of the eclipse swept towards us over Plymouth Sound, the gently enveloping darkness giving an ethereal quality to the crags of the tor.

As you return to the car you will notice that another splendid tor has joined the northern skyline. Great Mis Tor and its companion, tiny Little Mis, face the

Pew Tor

Staple Tor ridge across the River Walkham. An excellent view of all these tors and the lovely river between can be seen from the car park on the side of Merrivale Hill where Roos Tor at the end of the Staple Tor ridge is also visible. The tumbled rocks just outside the enclosure wall on the opposite side of the road are known as Over Tor.

From Merrivale the road crosses Merrivale Common, a lovely stretch of moorland to walk for views north and south and for exploration of the excellent Bronze Age double stone row, easily seen from the car when you are travelling in the other direction. Dartmoor has many similar antiquities and you will find informative leaflets on these and many other interesting features of the moor at the National Park Visitor Centres, including the one at Postbridge at the end of this excursion.

On the right hand side of the road, a grove of trees which once sheltered a school but is now Four Winds car park is a good starting point for exploration of the Common or simply a place for a closer view of the tors to the south. Below the mast is Hollow Tor with Billy's Tor further along the hill. The spoiltips you can see beyond Yellowmead Farm on the side of the hill are those from the quarry at Foggintor. A few ruins are all that remain of a sizeable village, built to house quarry workers. People lived here for over a 100 years, the last cottages being demolished in 1953. Quarrying reduced nearby Swell Tor to a mere shell, although Kings Tor in the foreground remains a sizeable tor despite its granite workings.

As the B3357 continues towards Two Bridges, a line of trees appears on the left hand side of the road. A side road branches off beyond a cattle grid, running north behind the trees out to the military flagpole near Holming Beam where there is a small carpark. From here there is an excellent view north to the head of the Cowsic valley where you can just make out the low stacks of Conies Down Tor on the hill to the left of the river. On the opposite side and closer is Lydford Tor with Crow Tor behind it in the dip before the ground rises to the Beardown Tors.

On your return to the B3357, continue towards Two Bridges. You will see Beardown Farm in its sheltered position below the Beardown Tors in the valley above the Cowsic's confluence with the West Dart River at Two Bridges. As you climb the hill beyond the hotel take the left fork onto the B3212 towards Postbridge. The tumbled rocks of Crockern Tor stand close to the road, accessible by a gate just beyond Parson's Cottage. From the early 14th Century, tinners assembled amongst the rocks here to make and amend the laws that governed their trade. Known as the Great Court or Stannary Parliament, this tradition continued into the early 18th Century, the last recorded Parliament being held on September 23rd 1703.

Further along the road the chimneys of the old gunpowder factory stand beside the picturesque collection of old cottages which form the hamlet of Powder Mills with its popular pottery. A fine array of Dartmoor heights forms the background here with firstly the Littaford Tors, then the cone of Longaford Tor further along the ridge and lastly Higher White Tor, all of them lying above the West Dart valley.

Longaford Tor beyond Powder Mills Cottages

On the right hand side of the road, Bellever Tor rises above the plantations which surround it. It is easily approached via the trackway which leads from the little car park beside the bridge across the Cherry Brook. As the road climbs out of the valley and runs along beside the Bellever plantations, little Arch Tor can be seen on the ridge on the left hand side and, as you dip into the valley of the East Dart, across the river Hartland Tor shelters the lovely house known as Hartyland.

To the visitor, Postbridge may seem like a hamlet strung out on either side of the road, but it hides a thriving community of warm and friendly people and an excellent National Park Visitor Centre to help you in your explorations here.

EXCURSIONS THROUGH NORTH DARTMOOR

NORTHERN SECTOR MAP

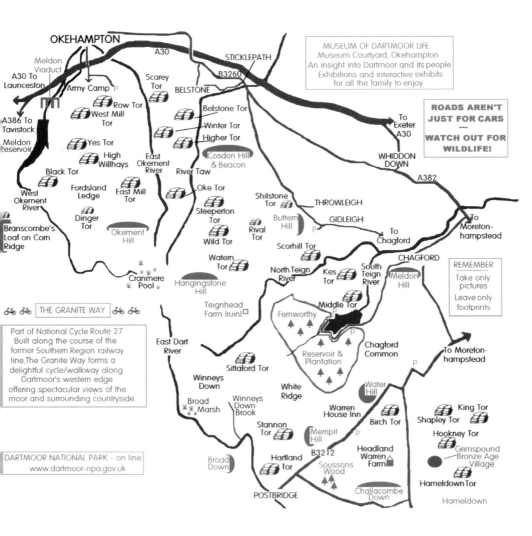

MUSEUM OF DARTMOOR LIFE
Museum Courtyard, Okehampton
An insight into Dartmoor and its people
Exhibitions and interactive exhibits
for all the family to enjoy

ROADS AREN'T JUST FOR CARS

WATCH OUT FOR WILDLIFE!

THE GRANITE WAY

Part of National Cycle Route 27
Built along the course of the
former Southern Region railway
line, The Granite Way forms a
delightful cycle/walkway along
Dartmoor's western edge
offering spectacular views of the
moor and surrounding countryside.

REMEMBER
Take only
pictures
Leave only
footprints

DARTMOOR NATIONAL PARK - on line
www.dartmoor-npa.gov.uk

On the days when Okehampton Range is to be used for live firing red flags will be flying from the prominent tors by 9 a.m. April to September or 10 a.m. October to March.You can check by 'phoning Freephone 0800 4584868.

Okehampton, home to the excellent Museum of Dartmoor Life, is the starting point for this excursion. From the traffic lights at the West end of Fore Street (High Street) turn into George Street which runs between the White Hart Inn and the National Westminster Bank. Turn right into Station Road (signposted Camp) and continue uphill, keeping right at the fork. This little road crosses both the railway line and the A30 before coming onto open moorland near the Army Camp. Bear left to pass the Sentry Box and cross the cattle grid onto the moor and over the bridge. The road climbs steadily and passes ample parking areas on your right but keep going until a stony track leaves the tarmac on the left and we suggest you park at the space available at the top of this track as the view opens out considerably at this point.

The track heads in an easterly direction where a magnificent array of tors command the skyline. Farthest left is Tors End Tor, (not marked on the Ordnance Survey Outdoor Leisure 28). The following peaks along the ridge are simply known as the Belstone Tors which are separated from Higher Tor by a ruined wall which climbs the hillside. This wall, which goes all the way down to the River Taw on the other side, is known as Irishman's Wall and formed a futile attempt by an Irishman in the early 19th Century to 'enclose' a large section of moor here for his own purposes. He apparently employed Irishmen to do the work and very hard it must have been too. However, the local moormen had no intention of losing their rights to graze stock here and they damaged the wall to such an extent that it was rendered useless and no attempt at repair was ever made although it remains a notable landmark.

The distinct peak of Winter Tor stands on the hillside below the ridge as it continues south, past a small rock pile known as Knattaborough, to Oke Tor whose main stacks are hidden from view by the trees at Hartor Farm. To the right of the trees is Steeperton Tor with its army hut and flagpole and you will also see the low mass of Hartor close to the road from which the farm takes its name. Continuing right is a long hill crowned by the multi stacks of East Mill Tor. Along the prominent ridge which runs north to the obvious height of Yes Tor (2030ft, 619m) lies High Willhays, the highest point on Dartmoor at 2039 feet (621m). Its low stacks, barely discernible from this distance, lie on the high point of the ridge and exceed Yes Tor by just nine feet. Further right the craggy summit of West Mill Tor and the lower stacks of Row Tor complete this scene of moorland splendour. Row Tor is quite close to hand and easily reached from here or from the other

The Belstone Tors

Scarey Tor with Belstone Ridge in the background

parking areas you passed on the way.**

A favourite walk of ours is to follow the stony track east in the direction of the Belstone Tors. It descends towards the East Okement River at its confluence with the Black-a-ven Brook which tumbles down the hillside to the right of the track. Here bridges and paved fords cross both river and brook giving access to further exploration of the Belstone Tors. The river here is particularly beautiful and overlooked by Scarey Tor on its opposite bank.

**Note: It is possible to use any of the tarmac roads in this area when firing is not in progress but there are many deep potholes and rough, stony sections which make them somewhat hazardous so take great care if you decide to venture along them.

A visit to Belstone Village

Alternatively, the lovely village of Belstone with its excellent pub, The Tors, lies within easy distance of Okehampton via either the A30 towards Exeter or the B3260 towards Sticklepath – just follow the signs for Belstone. There is ample parking opposite the Village Hall and a short walk through the village and along the lane beside the public house will be rewarded by a superb view across the Taw Valley towards Cosdon Hill. Walks in Belstone Cleave and along the Taw valley to the moor are possible from here. For walks around the Belstone Tors take the road to Watchet Hill Moorgate which runs uphill past the Water Treatment Works. Limited parking is available here just before you reach the moorgate where many options for further exploration await you.

Belstone village

This excursion takes you down the narrow Devon lane which runs along the flank of Cosdon Hill from the outskirts of Sticklepath to Gidleigh and Throwleigh. Like most in this part of Dartmoor it is a rustic, picturesque lane where views are obscured by the hills themselves and it needs to be negotiated at a slow speed and with care. At your destination there will be a walk of about a quarter of a mile uphill to a magnificent view and any further explorations you choose to make.

Sticklepath can be reached via the B3260 which runs east from Okehampton and is signposted Whiddon Down, Sticklepath, Belstone or, alternatively, by turning off the A30 at the Belstone, Sticklepath, South Zeal turn-off. At this point in the journey the peaks of the Belstone Tors are clearly visible to the right. Continue through the village of Sticklepath towards Whiddon Down. Shortly after passing business premises on the right, take the minor road also on the right signposted Gidleigh and Throwleigh. Continue along this road passing a turning on the left to East Weeke and Gooseford and then over a little bridge. Take the right fork to Shilstone and Gidleigh after which you will pass Shilstone Tor on your right and ignore a turning left to Gidleigh. The road winds through the Ensworthy farms and at the next fork bear right for Scorhill and Creaber passing another signpost for Gidleigh on your left. Scorhill is your final destination so turn off right at the Scorhill signpost and continue to the moorgate where there is parking for about half a dozen cars.

The moorgate leads into a stoney 'stroll' between enclosure walls and we suggest you follow the main track uphill. Hills and tors come into view as you climb but the crest of the hill brings the superb view which is the object of this excursion. Behind your left shoulder and partly obscured by a copse of trees is Meldon Hill above the town of Chagford. Moving from left to right and when the atmosphere is clear you may be able to make out the great hill of Hameldown directly behind the square stack of Kes Tor which stands on the other side of the River Teign. To the right of Kes Tor, Fernworthy Plantation dominates the horizon followed by the misty peak of Sittaford Tor with the trees which surround the lonely ruins of Teignhead Farm on the adjacent hillside. Walls climb this hillside, marking the limits of the farm and to the right of them along the ridge stand the stacks of Watern Tor, the two northern piles forming a distinct 'avenue' known as the Thurlestone. Like many of the weird and wonderful rock formations on Dartmoor this was formed by the agencies of wind and weather which have eroded the softer rock, leaving twin towers of layered granite 'pancakes'.

Wild Tor is next right and then across the Steeperton Brook you will see Steeperton Tor recognisable from many parts of the moor by its square hut with a flagpole close by. Moving right is the small peak of Round Tor which is marked on the Ordnance Survey Leisure 28 as Hound Tor (not to be confused with Great Hound Tor near Widecombe). Next comes Kennon Hill and then the great dome of Cosdon, its cairn barely visible in the haze on our last visit.

Kes Tor

Scorhill Tor

Over the crest of the hill Scorhill Tor comes into view to the left on its own hill beside the River Teign. Should you decide to follow it further, the main track will lead you down to one of the finest Bronze Age stone circles on the moor. Many of the smaller circles contain a grave, the circle of stones being the surviving part of the funeral mound. However Scorhill Circle and others like it have no grave but excavations have revealed a prolific amount of charcoal and these larger circles have consequently been termed ceremonial circles. Were they used to cremate the dead, to celebrate the harvest or the coming of Spring? Their purpose remains a Dartmoor mystery, adding to the interest and atmosphere of this beautiful moorland.

Chagford is not far away should you chose to visit it instead of returning the way you came. Turn right instead of left at the bottom of the little Scorhill road and follow the signs to Chagford. For several years we spent holidays here before we moved to Devon and as soon as we had thrown everything out of the car we headed for Meldon Hill and sometimes a sunset view of the moor. It can be approached via New Street which branches to the right off the Square near the Globe Inn opposite the church. Follow the road uphill and take the side road on the right just beyond Meldon Hall. Climbing steadily you will find limited parking in a layby at the crest of the hill where a track climbs to the rock stacks and trig pillar. Why this is not listed as a tor we don't know as it certainly resembles one! The view however is not in dispute, the tors you can see are similar but a little more distant than the hilltop at Scorhill.

Scorhill stone cicrle

MORETONHAMPSTEAD - WARREN HOUSE INN - PIZWELL
GRIMSPOUND - RETURN TO MORETON

This journey begins in Moretonhampstead, one of the 'gateways' to Dartmoor on the eastern side of the moor. From the town take the B3212 west towards Postbridge and Princetown, passing the Miniature Pony Centre on the way. The road winds beneath Dartmoor's eastern hills, but it is only when you cross the cattle grid and climb the hill onto the moor that any tors come into view. Your first destination is the large car park on the right hand side at the top of the hill where a number of tors on the eastern side of the moor can be identified providing, of course, that visibility is clear.

Looking north, Meldon Hill, is prominently in view just off the moor. Moving westward the square stack of Kes Tor stands above Middle Tor on the lower hillside and sometimes it is even possible to make out Frenchbeer Rock just beneath it. Hills, with and without rock stacks, range along the far horizon, but from here with the naked eye it is difficult to identify any other than Steeperton Tor with its square hut.

Turn right as you leave the car park and continue towards Postbridge. As the road bends to crest the last hill before the Warren House Inn, Fernworthy Forest, surrounding another of Dartmoor's reservoirs, tops the hills on the right hand side and the stacks of Birch Tor come into view on the left. Close to the left hand side of the road you will see an ancient cross, Bennett's Cross, and beyond it is a car park which we suggest you pull into.

The hillsides here are deeply scored by the tin mining gullies of the Birch Tor and Vitifer and the Golden Dagger Mines, the latter almost hidden in the conifers of Soussons Wood. Tin has been taken from Dartmoor for hundreds of years and mining only ceased here in the early part of the twentieth century. Birch Tor overlooks this once-busy valley from the east, its stacks dwarfed by the great ridge of Hameldown. To the south east the distant tops of Yar Tor and Corndon disappear into the mist whilst closer to hand is Bellever Tor surrounded by its plantations. Today this is a particularly beautiful scene in August as the hills in this part of the moor are swathed in purple heather which softens the contours and deep shadows of the gullies. The incentive to linger is further encouraged by the presence of the nearby Warren House Inn, where a home-cooked meal and real ale add to the enjoyment considerably.

Continuing towards Postbridge, the peak of Longaford Tor and Higher White Tor, recognisable from afar by the wall which bisects it, appear on the horizon. As the road descends Merripit Hill and dips into the valley of the East Dart, take the minor road on the left hand side signposted Widecombe. It is narrow and winding and along it are several homes and working farms, so take care.

Runnage Bridge crosses the Walla Brook between the ancient farms of Pizwell and Runnage, just two of the local farms which produce home-reared Dartmoor beef. In an alcove in Soussons Forest beside the road you will be able to take a close look at a stone circle with traces of the kistvaen and the cairn which once covered it. As the road leaves the forest behind, Hameldown's long ridge stretches across the skyline. Mounting its side is the Beech Hedge, something of a landmark in itself and the 'pimple' to the right of it is Hameldown Beacon. Continue down the hill and take the left turn at Grendon Bridge. Your road now runs between Challacombe Down on your left and Hameldown on your right. At the junction near Challacombe Farm turn left and soon Birch Tor will come into view on your left and Hookney Tor on your right. Headland Warren Farm can be seen in the valley also on the left. Drive past the entrance road and round the bend beyond it and park in the layby where there is room for about four cars. The Bronze Age village of Grimspound is your destination and this lies at the end of the well-worn path which you will see mounting the hill on the other side of the road. It is but a short walk to reach it crossing the little Grims Lake on the way.

Hut circle, Grimspound

This settlement may have been occupied intermittently at any time between 2,000 BC and 500BC but no exact date can be ascertained. When Grimspound was built, man had already occupied the moor for centuries as the climate was warmer and dryer than it is today, making it a more inviting place to live. Many of the trees had disappeared and the ever-abundant granite had become the main source of building material. Pioneer archaeologists, members of the Dartmoor Exploration Committee, carried out a thorough excavation of the site in 1894/5. They cleared the huts of debris and their partial restoration work here is still a valuable contribution to our knowledge of these people today .

The view from the village reaches far and wide. On a day of good visibility Laughter and Bellever Tors appear to the left of Challacombe Down, which is the long hill immediately in front you, and we believe the 'pimple' on the distant ridge must be Combestone Tor. North Hessary TV Mast and Princetown itself are also visible and you may even be able to make out the tower of St Michael's Church, Princetown on the right hand edge of the trees. Next right a cluster of tors appears on the horizon – firstly, the group with the flagpole is the Beardown Tors with Crow Tor tucked between Beardown and Longaford Tor. To the right of Longaford Tor is Higher White Tor. Nearer to hand, the white buildings of the Warren House Inn stand out against the hillside, with the cairn on Water Hill visible on the right hand side.

Close by, and within easy walking distance is Hookney Tor on the right (north) and should you climb the steep rocky pathway to the left (south) you will find yourself near the trig pillar on Hameldown Tor. From there a long, but easy, ridge walk with spectacular views will take you past some large Bronze Age barrows to Hameldown Beacon .

On your return to the car continue along the road to Challacombe Cross and then turn right onto the main B3212 for Moretonhampstead or left if you wish to go towards Postbridge.

Hookney Tor from Grimspound

EXCURSIONS THROUGH EAST DARTMOOR

EAST SECTOR MAP

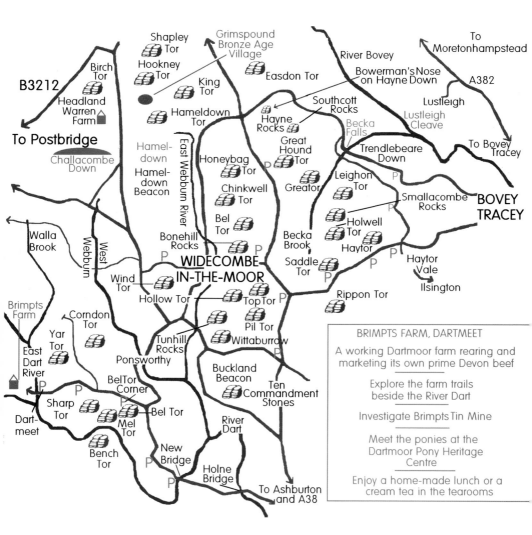

Shapley Tor
Grimspound Bronze Age Village
Birch Tor
Hookney Tor
Easdon Tor
River Bovey
Bowerman's Nose on Hayne Down
To Moretonhampstead
A382
B3212
King Tor
Headland Warren Farm
Hameldown Tor
Southcott Rocks
Lustleigh
Lustleigh Cleave
To Postbridge
Hayne Rocks
Becka Falls
To Bovey Tracey
Challacombe Down
Hameldown
Great Hound Tor
Trendlebeare Down
Honeybag Tor
Hameldown Beacon
East Webburn River
Chinkwell Tor
Greator
Leighon Tor
Smallacombe Rocks
BOVEY TRACEY
Bel Tor
Walla Brook
Holwell Tor
Becka Brook
Bonehill Rocks
Haytor
Haytor Vale
West Webburn
Webburn
WIDECOMBE-IN-THE-MOOR
Saddle Tor
Ilsington
Wind Tor
Hollow Tor
Top Tor
Rippon Tor
Brimpts Farm
Corndon Tor
Pil Tor
Yar Tor
Tunhill Rocks
Wittaburrow
East Dart River
Ponsworthy
Buckland Beacon
Dart-meet
Bel Tor Corner
Ten Commandment Stones
Sharp Tor
Bel Tor
River Dart
Mel Tor
Bench Tor
New Bridge
Holne Bridge
To Ashburton and A38

BRIMPTS FARM, DARTMEET

A working Dartmoor farm rearing and marketing its own prime Devon beef

Explore the farm trails beside the River Dart

Investigate Brimpts Tin Mine

Meet the ponies at the Dartmoor Pony Heritage Centre

Enjoy a home-made lunch or a cream tea in the tearooms

BOVEY TRACEY TO THE WIDECOMBE TORS

A number of spectacular and easily accessible tors crown the hills encircling the Vale of Widecombe and the picturesque village of Widecombe-in-the-Moor. This journey begins in the moorland town of Bovey Tracey which you leave by the B3387 towards Widecombe and Manaton. Shortly after passing the Dartmoor National Park Headquarters at Parke on the right hand side, take the left fork (B3387) signposted Haytor and Widecombe.

Haytor

The narrow, winding road climbs steadily to reach open moorland and then a bend in the road brings your first view of Haytor, from this angle resembling the knuckles on a clenched fist. A new National Park Visitor Centre lies adjacent to the car park at the bottom of the hill but our first detour begins from the large car park at the top of the hill opposite Haytor itself.

An easy climb brings you to the tor where rough steps can be used with care to climb the eastern outcrop; the western outcrop is known as Low Man. Views are magnificent in all directions. Facing south, towards the sea, little Bag Tor stands within its own enclosure and Rippon Tor marks the skyline. Close by, beside the road and also very accessible, is Saddle Tor and the low stacks of Emsworthy Rocks. Facing north, low mounds and spoil tips mark the quarry where, in the 1820s, granite was taken for New London Bridge and important buildings such as the British Museum. Holwell Tor, which can be seen behind Emsworthy Rocks, was also extensively quarried for granite and a tramway, its granite rails still in place, carried the stone off the moor. Holwell Tor and Smallacombe Rocks to the north overlook the deep little valley of the Becka Brook. Facing them and reached by a bridge across the brook the jagged rocks of Greator are dominated by the stacks of Great Hound Tor on the skyline.

Ample parking is available at several points along the road west from Haytor. Passing beneath Saddle Tor on the right and Rippon Tor on the left, Top Tor comes into view ahead as you reach the cattlegrid at Hemsworthy Gate. Take the road that goes off to the left under Rippon Tor (signposted Ashburton). Pil Tor lies a short distance south of Top Tor and yet another tor, Tunhill Rocks, lies hidden from view behind the cairn and stacks of Wittaburrow. Blackslade Mire lies between them and the road on which you are travelling, but this can be a crossed by a ford beneath Wittaburrow accessed by a track from the car park a little farther along the road.

Ahead and to the right a hill, crowned by a 'pimple', has been in view since Hemsworthy Gate. This is Buckland Beacon and is your next destination. Passing a crossroads and car park on your right, the road climbs to a cattle grid with a parking area on the left hand side.

Cross the road and follow the track to the wall corner before turning left. The wall and track will lead you to Buckland Beacon and yet another magnificent panorama. Beneath the tumble of rocks on the south side the beautiful Holne Chase Woods sweep down towards the Dart and beyond. Rippon Tor, Saddle Tor and Haytor mark the northern skyline, whilst closer to hand the churches of Buckland-in-the Moor and Leusdon stand amongst the scattering of homes, farms and multi-coloured fields which characterise this delightful part of Devon. On a clear day you may be able to pick out the point of Sharp Tor above Dartmeet and the television mast on North Hessary Tor.

This eastern buttress of Dartmoor was one of the traditional beacon hills where fires were lit to send messages quickly from one end of the country to the other. It is said that a fire was lit on Buckland Beacon in 1588 to signal the sighting of the Spanish Armada.

Close to the main outcrop lie two large slabs of granite inscribed with the Ten Commandments which were commissioned in 1928 by William Whitley, Lord of the Manor of Buckland, to celebrate the rejection by Parliament of a controversial revision to the Book of Common Prayer.

On your return to the car it is possible to continue down the hill to Ashburton but, assuming that you wish to continue exploring, we suggest you return to Hemsworthy Gate and turn left, bearing right at the next fork towards Great Hound Tor which you can see on the right hand side. As you proceed a line of tors will come into view on your left commencing with Bonehill Rocks which are easily accessed by a little road which goes off left from the one you are on. It leads to parking areas close to the rocks and also gives access to Bell Tor, Chinkwell Tor and the craggy stacks of Honeybag Tor at the far end of the ridge. Views over the Widecombe valley towards Hameldown and beyond are magnificent.

The Ten Commandment Stones, Buckland Beacon

The Honeybag ridge comes fully into view as you continue towards the spectacular rock stacks of Great Hound Tor, Viewed from a distance its shape is said to resemble a pack of hounds chasing over the hill. Immortalised by the legendary Sherlock Holmes in Hound of the Baskervilles, its close proximity to the road makes it a popular place. When your road bends to the left at a junction, take the right fork and find the large car park where an excellent refreshment van stands each day during the summer. The easy climb to the tor will reward you with yet another magnificent view. To the north is Hayne Down where Hayne Rocks and Southcott Rocks cover the top of the hill. Here below the crest on the west side stands a tall rock stack known as Bowerman's Nose. Resembling a man, frozen in time, it gazes forever towards the little town of Chagford and was described by Dartmoor poet, Noel Carrington, as 'a granite idol'. Easdon Tor can also be seen on the hill beyond Hayne Down.

Great Hound Tor

South is Rippon Tor and the sea and paths lead from Hound Tor down to the Becka Brook and Hound Tor Combe, passing the jagged piles of Greator Rocks where, in late spring, a mist of bluebells sweeps the slopes spreading in swathes across the valley. Here too on a sheltered hillside, are the ruins of a medieval village. Recognisable are the longhouses where animals and humans lived together under a thatched roof of straw, heather or reed. Even the corn-drying barns with their tiny ovens have survived the centuries and these interesting relics of a bygone age are carefully conserved by National Park archaeologists.

Bowerman's Nose

Across the valley the steep hillside rises to a magnificent ridge commencing from the point where cairn-topped Black Hill climbs from a patchwork of green fields. Further along the massive rocks of Leighon Tor and Smallacombe Rocks tumble in disarray down the hillside and the black face of the quarry beneath Holwell Tor leads the eye to the distinctive rocks of Haytor high on the skyline. You will soon find it easy to recognise Haytor in the distance from other parts of the moor

We suggest you return along the road, passing the Bonehill junction on your right and then make the awkward right turn onto Widecombe Hill. The car park on your right at the top of the hill offers a short easy walk north to Bonehill Rocks or across the road to Top Tor to the south and its close neighbour, Pil Tor which is not in view from here. As you continue downhill towards the village, car parks on the left hand side access paths which lead across the hillside towards Hollow Tor and Tunhill Rocks.

Widecombe village has much to offer its visitors: ample parking and all facilities including a National Trust shop and a beautiful church. Even when the village is busy the churchyard retains its essential element of peace and tranquillity and views of the tors on its eastern skyline are excellent. Exploring the little lanes surrounding Widecombe does, however, require great care as they are narrow, one track roads with passing places where speed is limited.

Bonehill Rocks

Short diversion from Widecombe

From the main car park in Widecombe turn right and then left onto the road towards Ponsworthy. Go downhill past the Post Office and then pass the school on your right hand side. Take the steep road to Southcombe which appears on the right. This climbs onto the open moor on a 'saddle' between Hameldown on the right and Wind Tor on the left and turn into the car park on the right hand side of the road. A short walk option would be the rocks of Wind Tor but for spectacular views on both sides of Hameldown we suggest you follow the wide green paths which head north from the car park.

Across Widecombe Vale the little fields of this fertile valley spread upwards from the village to the line of tors and rock stacks on the far side. Hollow Tor and Tunhill Rocks can be seen above the enclosures on the hillside with Top Tor and Pil Tor higher on the ridge. The steep road up Widecombe Hill divides these tors from those of the Honeybags ridge which stretches away to the left. The road seems to lead to Haytor itself which, from a certain point on this pathway, appears to stand at the crest of the hill. Further right on the skyline is Rippon Tor with Buckland Beacon on the far end of the ridge.

Passing the walls of Kingshead Farm the track climbs to Hameldown Beacon. Far to the west the television mast on North Hessary Tor marks Princetown at its foot whilst Corndon Tor is just a small hump on a long ridge closer to hand. Immediately west the farms in the valley of the West Webburn River lead the eye to Challacombe Down with the isolated Warren House Inn beyond it on the Postbridge road. Because of the broadness of the hill, a short detour across Old House Hill to the east is necessary to look over the Widecombe valley, but this also provides an excellent view over the massive rocks and multi-stacks of Honeybag Tor.

Your excursion can be continued along the ridge path to Hameldown Tor and Grimspound . On the way you will pass four earthen Bronze Age barrows one of which yielded to archaeologists a beautifully crafted dagger pommel, carved from amber and inlaid with many tiny gold pins, a rare find in Dartmoor's peaty soil. The much corroded blade lay a short distance away. Dating these sepulchres is often an impossible task, but I like to think that in this high place the chieftains of the Grimspound village found their final resting place.

Overlooking Widecombe from Dunstone Down

ASHBURTON TO DARTMEET

This journey covers the short section of the B3357 Tavistock to Ashburton road which runs from Ashburton to Dartmeet signposted from Ashburton as Princetown and Dartmeet. Once again, care is needed as it is narrow and winding if picturesque. It crosses one side of a giant loop in the River Dart at Holne Bridge and then climbs steeply, passing a by-road to Holne village near the entrance to the Holne Chase Hotel, before descending again to cross the other side of the loop at New Bridge. Here there is ample parking and riverside walks, plus a National Park Visitor Centre. The road is wider from here, but climbs steeply up New Bridge Hill where parking is available on either side of the road at the top at one end of what is known as Dr Blackall's Drive which we will explore briefly further on. Drive carefully through the village of Poundsgate and continue up the hill. A road on the right provides an alternative route to Widecombe. The main Princetown/ Dartmeet road continues to climb through the hedges, with glimpses of Bel Tor on your left, until it crosses a cattle grid and comes onto open moorland at Bel Tor Corner. Your first diversion commences from the large car park on your left.

Looking north east a wide panorama encompasses Buckland Beacon on the far right, Rippon Tor – the tallest on the skyline, Haytor with Saddle Tor close by. Next comes Bonehill Rocks, Bell Tor, Chinkwell and Honeybag Tors and the great whale-back ridge of Hameldown. Beyond them in the far distance Fernworthy Forest caps the hilltops. Closer to hand is Corndon Down and Corndon Tor with Yar Tor behind it, whilst closer still is Sharp Tor with the little tree in the cleft at the top. Bel Tor itself lies in an enclosure nearby.

From the car park face south and follow the path which runs close to the wall on your left and then turn left down a trackway which goes between the enclosure walls. This is the start of Dr Blackall's Drive, which was created by Dr Thomas Blackall in the 1880s so that guests to his Manor House at nearby Spitchwick could enjoy the beautiful scenery on his country estate from the comfort of a carriage. It leaves the enclosures at the foot of Mel Tor which stands high above the Dart gorge and continues along the ridge to the top of New Bridge Hill.

Mel Tor's upper stacks are just a short walk away and always seem to me to be on the point of toppling down the slope to the river far below. Until the 1950s the old local custom of rolling flaming wagon wheels down the hillside took place here on Midsummer's Day, the object being to reach the river, although the woods and outcrops littering the way must have impeded their progress considerably.

On the summit of the main outcrop are four superb rock basins, each with a lip worn away by the water which gathers in them after heavy rain. There are many such basins on the moor, all formed by water wearing away the softer rock, although once upon a time they were thought to be the handiwork of the Druids.

Mel Tor rock basins

This is a place to linger and enjoy the view. Across the gorge stands Bench or Benji Tor, the summit rocks almost insignificant from here, but on its east side sheer cliffs reach down to the trees above the winding river. Further west the rocks of Combestone Tor can be seen beside the Venford Reservoir road. Nearer to hand Sharp Tor crowns the hillside where Rowbrook House stands on a shelf above the gorge, surely one of the most magnificently sited homes in England.

On your return to the car, turn left from the car park and continue along the main road until you are adjacent with Sharp Tor on your left. On your right a by-road leads uphill crossing another which comes up from the main road a little further along. Follow the signpost uphill towards Sherwell and find a parking space near where tracks go up to tors on both sides of the road. On the left is Yar Tor and an easy climb to the top brings you to a cairn and rock stacks overlooking the deep valley of the East Dart with Brimpts Farm on the hillside.

On the right side of the road another track goes up to Corndon Tor. Beside it stands a modern memorial known as Cave-Penny Cross, erected to the memory of Evelyn Anthony Cave-Penny who lived in the hamlet of Sherwell and was killed at the age of eighteen in Palestine in 1918. Once at the top, a long walk follows the ridge between the rock stacks with far reaching views over the valley to Hameldown and the tors above Widecombe which you may be able to identify from previous viewpoints on this journey. Walking north brings the hamlets of

Sharp Tor above Dartmeet

Sherwell and Babeny into view in their little valley and on a clear day it is possible to see a white building against the hillside far away to the north-west. This is the Warren House Inn on the Postbridge to Moretonhampstead Road.

Returning to the main road a left turn takes you back to Ashburton and a right turn brings you to the top of Dartmeet Hill and on to the large car park at Dartmeet, where there are walks beside the river and the Badgers Holt tearooms. The Pixie Shop lies up the hill on the other side of the river close to the access road to Brimpts Farm with its farm walks, summertime tearooms and the Dartmoor Pony Heritage Centre.

Cave Penny Cross below Corndon Tor

EXCURSIONS THROUGH SOUTH DARTMOOR

SOUTHERN SECTOR MAP

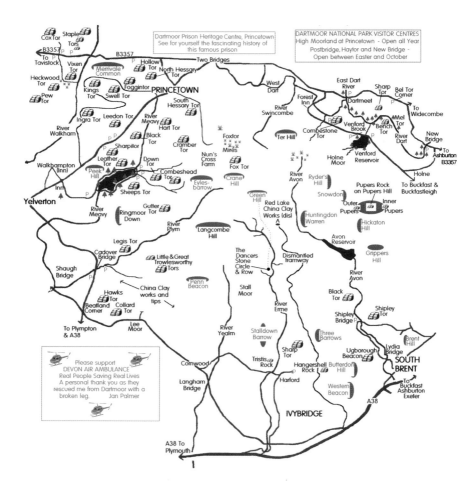

PRINCETOWN TO YELVERTON

This excursion begins in Princetown, home to Dartmoor National Park's major Visitor Centre, where you can take in a film about the moor in the little theatre, browse the books, audios and pictorial displays or glean information from the friendly and knowledgeable staff.

Leave Princetown on the B3212 towards Yelverton, an unfenced road across open moorland frequented by grazing animals, so take extra care. The television mast on North Hessary Tor dominates the scene on the right hand side of the road. Beneath it runs the trackway of the old Princetown to Yelverton Railway popular with walkers and cyclists. In front, from left to right, the skyline is dominated by Leather Tor and Sharpitor which seem to tower above Black Tor on the lower skyline. Then come the multiple stacks of Leedon Tor and farthest right, almost in the background, is Ingra Tor. As the ground dips at Devil's Bridge to cross the headwaters of the River Meavy, Hart Tor appears on the left not too far from road. On the ridge beyond it stands the square nobble of Cramber Tor and the large hump of Sheepstor joins the skyline behind Leather Tor.

Black Tor lies close to the left hand side of the road and is easily approachable from a lay-by just beyond it. A couple of parking areas on this stretch of road also give access to Leedon Tor which is now prominent on the right hand skyline.

The logan stone on Black Tor

A favoured excursion along this road is from the car park close to the pond beneath Sharpitor. On a clear day the view westward is spectacular. If you are already familiar with the western side of the moor you will have no difficulty in identifying Brentor Church in the far distance. Directly below it Pew Tor can be seen with Pew Tor Cottage at its foot. Cox Tor, the Staple Tor ridge and Roos Tor, Great and Little Mis Tors range the skyline. In the Walkham valley to the left of the dip between Cox and Staple Tors lies Vixen Tor; Ingra Tor is on the opposite side of the river, with King Tor just below the skyline. The influence of sunlight at different times of the day or year, cloud formations, the clarity of the atmosphere all make a marked difference to the magnificent scenery you will find everywhere. With this in mind we suggest you climb the rough path to Sharpitor. Height too will widen the horizons and if you pause and turn as you climb the hill, yet another tor, Great Links, has joined the distant skyline.

At the top make your way carefully across the rocky ground to admire the equally magnificent view on the other side. A large part of southern Dartmoor lies before you and the reservoir in the Meavy valley below is perhaps one of the most beautiful in England. Close at hand the steep rocks of Leather Tor tumble down the hillside and beyond the reservoir, Sheepstor dominates the view, its rock stacks mirrored in the calm waters on a tranquil day. Across the valley to the left rises Down Tor, with Combeshead Tor behind it on the right. The cliff-type peak to the right of an isolated copse of trees is Gutter Tor and farther to the right, the conical peak of Hen Tor stands below Langcombe Hill. On the far horizon further south you may be able to make out the crags of Great Trowlesworthy Tor and the white slopes of the china clay pits.

Leather Tor from Sharpitor

From Sharpitor good tracks lead along the hillside past Peek Hill to Lowery Tor on a lower hillside. Seasonal colour gives an ever-changing view from snow on the tops, to a sprinkling of blue in the woodland clearings; to the fresh young green of early summer through to the red-brown of the bracken and the trees in their autumn splendour.

Burrator Reservoir is easily reached by continuing along the B3212 towards Yelverton and turning left at the Burrator Inn, then left again to the dam (along the road signposted Sheepstor). Here a delightful but tiny road circles the reservoir with parking opportunities and easy access to moorland walks and the lakeside paths. Popular though it is, an ice-cream van (and toilets) near the dam are the only tourist amenities here, anything else could put this unspoilt yet fragile beauty at risk and disturb the atmosphere of real tranquility which epitomises this lovely lake and its ring of majestic tors.

Across Burrator Reservoir to Sheepstor

Once again your journey begins in Princetown on the B3212, this time towards Two Bridges with a splendid view of the town and the Prison beneath North Hessary Tor. Great Mis Tor appears on the left skyline with the Beardown Tors ahead beside the plantation. Ever-changing views of Bellever Tor will accompany you as you turn right onto the B3357 at Two Bridges to cross the West Dart River and continue towards Ashburton. The road dips to cross the Cherry Brook and climbs again towards Dunnabridge offering parking areas for walks over to Bellever and its neighbour, Laughter Tor. For the purposes of this journey however we suggest you pull into the car park on the right hand side before the road dips again to cross the brook at Dunnabridge. Park with Bellever Tor behind you and look to the left-hand end of the long line of hills which has been in view on your right since leaving Two Bridges. A group of low rock stacks is now visible on the skyline, marking Combestone Tor and your destination. It stands in a prime position above the Dart Gorge, overlooking the confluence of the East and West Dart rivers at Dartmeet.

Bellever Tor

To reach it continue along the B3357. A small tor, Huccaby Tor, stands in the enclosure just before you reach Brimpts Plantation but is only visible when you are driving in the opposite direction. Then turn right towards Hexworthy and Venford Reservoir. The road is narrow with many twists and turns so take care, especially when you cross the tiny bridge over the West Dart and head uphill around some sharp hairpin bends to the Forest Inn which is an excellent and welcoming hostelry. Continue up the hill, ignoring the turning to Sherberton, and proceed down the other side to Saddle Bridge which crosses the O Brook as it tumbles down to join the West Dart. Combestone Tor and car park lie close to the road at the top of the next hill and here you can stretch your legs around the tor and enjoy the magnificent panoramic views.

Combestone Tor

Out of sight on Combestone's north side flows Double Dart through its spectacular gorge which is accessible via the large car park at Dartmeet. Directly across the valley Yar Tor stands high above the river with Corndon Tor to the right. Soon after the confluence of the East and West Dart rivers at Dartmeet the river turns east and runs beneath the pinnacle of Sharp Tor. To the right on the same side of the Dart and literally overhanging the steep slope down to the river is Mel Tor which faces Bench or Benji Tor across the river. An excursion to Bench Tor is possible from the car park on the far side of Venford Reservoir where paths will lead you up the slope to where the multi stacks of the tor crown a steep sided ridge above the river. From this point the immense depth of the gorge is apparent and it is hard to believe that, as Dartmoor was never covered by ice sheets, it has been formed solely by the action of water.

From Combestone the eastern skyline is marked by the long ridge of Hameldown, the high point of Rippon Tor and the 'pimple' that marks Buckland Beacon.

To the west on a clear day the North Hessary mast and Great Mis Tor can be seen in the far background. The Beardown Tors mark the next ridge and then the peak of Longaford Tor and Higher White Tor. Closer to hand are Bellever and Laughter Tors which you passed on your journey here. Beyond them Dartmoor stretches as far as the eye can see to the hills capped by Fernworthy Forest.

Across the road to the south stretch southern Dartmoor's lonely hills with fewer rock stacks to catch the eye. Access to them is via tiny roads, sometimes with tall hedges and few passing places and it requires a much longer walk to reach the moor.

From Combestone Tor, as an alternative to returning by your outward route, the road continues to Venford Reservoir and then on to Holne where signposted roads lead to Buckfastleigh or back to the B3357 Ashburton road near the Holne Chase Hotel.

Dart Gorge from Combestone Tor

YELVERTON TO CADOVER BRIDGE.

From Yelverton roundabout take the minor road signposted Cadover Bridge and Meavy (mind the humps!) and continue towards Cadover Bridge. Sheepstor becomes ever prominent on the left hand side as you cross the River Meavy and as you climb the hill Leather Tor and Sharpitor come into view to the left of Sheepstor with the Staple Tors and Cox Tor in the distance. As the road twists towards Cadover Bridge you may be able to make out the point of Hen Tor in the distance on the left hand side and the more prominent Trowlesworthy Tors. Dominating the whole scene is the evidence of the China Clay works and even the older, 'landscaped', tips which are covered in a thin veil of vegetation look very out of place in this moorland setting.

Cross Cadover Bridge and turn immediately left along a minor road. On the left hand side are parking areas and a trackway to further parking close to the River Plym, a very popular riverside area in the summer. Continue along the minor road with care as it is frequented by lorries from the nearby Clay Works. The road continues beyond the entrance to the Works and ends at a car park with fine views of the nearby hills and tors. Below you is the little valley of the Blackaton Brook which joins the Plym near the car parks mentioned above. From right to left from this viewpoint Penn Beacon is the prominent hill to the east.

Little Trowlesworthy Tor with pink granite monument base

Next in line is Shell Top and then Great Trowlesworthy Tor followed by its partner Little Trowlesworthy. Legis Tor is in the foreground on the opposite side of the Plym. In the distance on a clear day you will see the television mast on

North Hessary Tor; to its right is Gutter Tor recognisable from this angle by the gap in the middle and even further away is Great Mis Tor. Moving left again is Sheepstor facing Leather Tor, Sharpitor and Peek Hill across Burrator Reservoir which is hidden in the valley. Far off the moor on the left hand side is Brentor Church on its conical hill.

Should you wish to continue your explorations towards South Brent, return to the main road at Cadover Bridge and turn left and continue to the crossroads at Beatland Corner. Turning right here would take you through the little village of Shaugh Prior to Shaugh Bridge where there is ample parking. Here you will find lovely riverside walks at the confluence of the Rivers Plym and Meavy. Turning left will take you through the hamlets of Wotter and Lee Moor, past little Whitehill Tor and through ancient woods to Cornwood and on to Lee Mill where a short stretch of the A38 will connect you to Ivybridge and South Brent for the following excursions.

Cadover Bridge

IVYBRIDGE TO HARFORD MOOR
and BITTAFORD TO WESTERN BEACON

Throughout Dartmoor's southern sector and the eastern sector from South Brent to Buckfastleigh, the open moor is reached by long stretches of the tiniest of Dartmoor lanes, with sometimes a considerable walk (1 mile or more) to reach a hilltop where the surrounding hills are identifiable. Bronze Age man was busy in this area and cairn-topped hills are more numerous than tors. The following three excursions are suggested bearing these factors in mind.

From the roundabout at the end of the sliproad off the A38 at Ivybridge follow the B3213 towards Bittaford. This will bypass the town centre bringing you to its outskirts. At a crossroads called Toll Bar Cross turn into Cole Lane, signposted Harford and Lukesland. It looks as if you're going into a housing estate but continue to a signpost named Stowford Bridge and continue towards Harford. At Combeshead crossroads take the Harford road once again and at Harford Church take the lane signposted Harford Moor. Park inside the Moorgate and with your back to the gate follow the track which heads uphill to the left. Keep to the higher track which bears off right as this is probably the easiest and quickest way to a suitable viewpoint. To your left is the valley of the beautiful River Erme and the little tor on the opposite side of the river is Tristis Rock. As you move uphill there are ever-increasing views across the South Hams to the sea. Close by, the great hill known as Stalldown Barrow dominates the far side of the river whilst further west in the distance Penn Beacon stands amidst the china clay tips.

Tristis Rock

Gradually the tip of a tor will come into view in front of you (north) as you climb. This is Sharp Tor and the way to it is easy should you wish to do so. A short distance to the right of it is what seems to be another tor as it has a rocky summit, but the rocks in fact belong to three ruined cairns, hence its name Three Burrows. According to Eric Hemery, a well-respected Dartmoor author, even the dome of Cut Hill on the northern moor can be seen from here on a clear day.

Winding between Sharp Tor and Three Barrows runs the trackbed of the Red Lake Tramway which for twenty years between 1911 and 1930 carried men, tools and supplies to Red Lake China Clay Works, 7½ miles into the moor. The clay itself was carried from the moor by means of a lengthy pipeline of which remnants still remain near Sharp Tor. If you have climbed high enough the view to the south will have opened up and you may be able to make out the line of the tramway as it passes the stack known as Hangershell Rock. East of Hangershell is Ugborough Beacon whilst beyond it to the south stands Butterdon Hill, again with three Bronze Age cairns on its summit and then Dartmoor's most southerly hill, Western Beacon, which also has a cairn.

Western Beacon and Butterdon Hill can be reached from the B3213 by continuing towards Bittaford until a tall works chimney appears on your left. On the far side of it is a tiny road beneath a narrow bridge which leads up to a moorgate where you will find limited parking at the roadside. Paths and tracks lead round and up the steep side of the Beacon.

Sharp Tor above the River Erme

42

From the A38 sliproad, follow the signs to South Brent village centre. However you enter the village you need to turn into Station Road signposted Didworthy and Avon Dam. Cross the bridge and continue up the hill and out of the village to a crossroads called Harbourneford Cross (name not visible on the side you will approach it) and turn left to Didworthy and Avon Dam. The little road climbs through the fields giving lovely views to nearby Brent Hill and the range of hills along Dartmoor's eastern edge. At Gingaford Cross turn left and then bear right at Bloody Pool Cross, following the sign to Shipley Bridge and Didworthy. As you near the bridge you will have a fine view of Shipley Tor rising behind the trees on the right hand side of the road. Unfortunately access to the tor is difficult as it is partly surrounded by private ground.

River Avon above Shipley Bridge

Adjacent to the large car park beside the bridge are the ruins of an old factory where an inflammable oil called naptha was once distilled from peat. Like many of Dartmoor's important relics these are looked after by the National Park. Especially appealing to all ages and abilities, is the stroll along the little tarmac road which follows the river all the way to the Avon dam. Easily accessed from the car park, it will take you along the steep sided gorge where ancient trees overhang the water. On the far bank the woods and fields of Shipley Farm climb the hillside beneath Shipley Tor.

There are many places to picnic beside this beautiful river as it flows down from the moor in a succession of waterslides, rapids and deep, tranquil pools. About a mile from the car park a succession of tumbled ruins beside the road are all that remain of Brentmoor House, a granite hunting lodge complete with stables and a coachhouse built in the 19th century. I have sat amongst the ruins many times as an elderly and recently deceased friend of mine regaled me with her happy childhood memories of holidays here when the old house was full of life and laughter.

Beyond the ruins a steep path through the bracken will take you up to the crumbling rocks of Black Tor and fine views of the valley and the surrounding hills. Further on a bridge crosses the river and the road continues on the far side to the dam. Just across the bridge, if you wish to do so, you should find paths which take you up the hill on that side of the river to Shipley Tor.

Shipley Tor

GAZETEER OF DARTMOOR TORS

	Height in Metres	Grid Ref.
Aish Tor	283	702 715
Arms Tor	457	541 863
Barn Hill Rocks	336	533 748
Beardown Tors	513	60 77
Bel Tor	354	697 730
Bell Tor (Widecombe)	412	730 778
Bellever Tor	443	644 764
Belstone Tors	479	61 92
Bench Tor	313	691 716
Billy's Tor	440	567 745
Birch Tor	487	687 814
Black Tor (Meavy)	335	573 718
Black Tor (Avon)	320	681 635
Black Tor (Okement)	488	567 895
Bonehill Rocks	393	731 774
Brai/Brat Tor	452	539 855
Buckland Beacon	390	735 731
Chinkwell Tor	458	728 781
Collard Tor	251	557 621
Combeshead Tor	371	587 688
Combestone Tor	350	670 718
Conies Down Tor	488	589 791
Corndon Tor	434	687 742
Cox Tor	442	531 762
Cramber Tor	418	583 711
Crockern Tor	404	615 757
Doe Tor	425	542 848
Down Tor	366	580 694
Easdon Tor	438	729 823
East Mill Tor	513	599 901
Feather Tor	313	535 741
Foggintor	412	567 735
Fur Tor	572	588 831
Ger Tor	412	547 831
Great Hound Tor	414	743 790
Great Links Tor	586	552 867
Great Mis Tor	538	562 769

	Height in Metres	Grid Ref.
Great Nodden	437	539 874
Great Staple Tor	455	542 760
Greator	371	751 791
Gutter Tor	350	578 669
Hameldown Tor	529	703 806
Hare Tor	537	551 842
Hart Tor	390	581 720
Hartland Tor	410	641 799
Hawks Tor	265	552 625
Haytor	457	758 769
Heckwood Tor	321	539 737
High Willhays	621	580 894
Higher Tor	466	612 917
Higher White Tor	522	620 786
Hollow Tor (Walkham)	472	571 745
Hollow Tor (Widecombe)	372	731 762
Honeybag Tor	445	729 787
Hookney Tor	497	699 813
Ingra Tor	338	555 721
Kes Tor	437	665 862
King Tor	488	709 816
Kings Tor	380	556 739
Laughter Tor	420	653 757
Leather Tor	366	563 700
Leedon Tor	389	563 719
Little Links Tor	518	547 869
Little Mis Tor	455	564 763
Little Staple Tor	383	538 753
Littaford Tors	466	615 771
Longaford Tor	507	616 779
Lowery Tor	335	556 698
Lydford Tor	514	599 781
Mel Tor	346	693 725
Middle Tor	410	669 858
Middle Staple Tor	431	540 756
North Hessary Tor	517	578 742
Oke Tor	466	612 900
Over Tor	381	558 753

	Height in Metres	Grid Ref.
Pew Tor	311	533 735
Pil Tor	348	735 759
Rippon Tor	473	747 756
Roos Tor	454	543 766
Row Tor	468	593 916
Saddle Tor	428	751 763
Scarey Tor	365	606 923
Scorhill Tor	343	658 871
Shapley Tor	487	669 821
Sharp Tor (Lyd)	519	550 848
Sharp Tor (Dart)	380	686 730
Sharp Tor (Erme)	414	649 617
Sharpitor	396	560703
Sheepstor	369	559 676
Sittaford Tor	538	633 830
Smallacombe Rocks	390	754 783
Stannon Tor	462	646 811
Steeperton Tor	532	618 888
Swell Tor	403	562 732
Top Tor	432	736 762
Tors End Tor	457	614 927
Tunhill Rocks	396	731 758
Ugborough Beacon	378	668 591
Vixen Tor	317	542 742
Watern Tor	526	29 868
West Mill Tor	500	587 909
White Tor	468	542 787
Wild Tor	531	623 877
Wind Tor	375	708 758
Winter Tor	427	609 915
Wittaburrow	403	753 752
Yar Tor	416	678 740
Yes Tor	619	581 902

Do you want to explore Dartmoor by car, getting to know many of the tors and their names? Would you like to combine your car journeys with a short walk or two to stretch your legs, get a bit of fresh air and discover the beauty and atmosphere of our glorious moorland? This little book will help you to do just that. The excursions within these pages name the major tors you will see from the road and parking areas. Short walks are included on the route to enable you to further enjoy the dramatic torscapes. Opportunities for further explorations and longer walks will, of course, occur on the way – the choice is yours.

Ossie and Janet Palmer have spent the last twelve years exploring, taking photographs and writing about Dartmoor. Many of their articles have appeared in local and County magazines. Their book *Let's Go Letterboxing – A Beginner's Guide* was published in 1998 and has enjoyed several reprints. It was followed by *Dartmoor Cameos* which recounted the lives of people they have come to know for whom Dartmoor is a very special place either through work, research or leisure activities. Ossie's little book of photographs, *Dartmoor - A Pictorial Souvenir*, is also available as a reminder of your journeys through the moor.

ORCHARD
PUBLICATIONS

9 781898 964841

£3.95